THE EIGHTH MOUNTAIN
POETRY PRIZE

THE EIGHTH MOUNTAIN POETRY PRIZE was established in 1988 in honor of the poets whose words envision and sustain the feminist movement, and in recognition of the major role played by women poets in creating the litera-ture of their time. Women poets world-wide are invited to participate. One manuscript is selected each year by a poet of national reputation. Publication and an advance of one thousand dollars are funded by a private donor. *The Eating Hill* was selected by Audre Lorde to be the first winner of the Eighth Mountain Poetry Prize.

THE EATING HILL

THE EATING HILL

Karen Mitchell

THE EIGHTH MOUNTAIN PRESS

PORTLAND · OREGON · 1989

"Where Have the Black Sheep Gone?" and "Visit" were originally published in *Obsidian;* "Birmingham, Alabama: 1963", "Returning", "For Michael", and "Tree Stillness" were originally published in *Open Places;* "On the Anniversary of Your Death" and "For John T. Allen" were originally published in *Ploughshares;* "Clara Bell" was originally published in *Southern Exposure;* and "Belly Edge", "The Eating Hill", "Sometimes", "The Paper Woman" and "Grandfather" were originally published in *13th Moon.*

The author wishes to thank members of the Mitchell family, Marilyn Hacker, Toni Cade Bambara, Donna Van Slyke, the MacDowell Colony, and "friends I have met along the way and friends who have gone before me."

"They Call it Stormy Monday, but Tuesday's Just as Bad", copyright © 1948, 1968 by Aaron T. Walker, used by permission of Gregmark Music, Inc.

Cover art: "The Ritual" by Gwendolyn Knight, collection of the University of Atlanta, courtesy of the artist and Francine Seders Gallery, photographed by Chris Eden

Cover design by Marcia Barrentine
Book design by Ruth Gundle

Library of Congress Cataloging-in-Publication Data
Mitchell, Karen L., 1955-
    The eating hill / Karen L. Mitchell. — 1st ed.
        p.   cm.
    ISBN0-933377-04-5 : $8.95
    I. Title.
    PS3563.I76745E2   1989
    811'.54—dc20   89-23631

The Eighth Mountain Press
624 Southeast 29th Avenue
Portland, Oregon 97214

for Michael

CONTENTS

For the Mourner

You sit at your simple breakfast
and expect them to answer you,
but they say nothing.
The dead will not tell you
of their eyes, all turning
into dust that blows away from you
even when you open the window
to let it in.
For the moment, you prefer
them to faces that can touch
any part of you.
You give those empty mouths
tongues to speak your language,
tongues to move
so that when they
tap your shoulder, you hear
your name.
And you look for them everywhere
until sound becomes your memory.
You look for them in closets that hold
nothing but worn-out dresses and
scarves that wrap around you and hold
you still,
on beaches that separate
shells from bodies becoming
lost in sand,
on streets curling up to you
when everything is moving
on yellow,
in sleep where you hear your voice

asking for something
more than the sun that dangles outside
your window—
but even then,
the dead dream themselves silent:
the dead do not talk,
even though you
hear them.

The Paper Woman

1

When he came home,
all sewn together from war,
she wore a paper hat,
stood over the casket
and watched his face,
hard and stiff;
she smoothed his shirt until
the wrinkles were as straight
as his hair mashed
against his head.
And then she told him
she liked the three dolls
he sent her for Christmas,
the three smiles laughing
at nothing but the grass
running backwards in sunlight.

2

I thought she would die
in the rain,
but she covered her curls
with newsprint
that later changed her hair
from gray to black;
she gave the preacher dollar bills
until her husband led her away
from the grave where she had
planted paper flowers
around his feet.

She was that crazy woman
who kept everything.
My father told me
to burn her trash that blew
into my mother's mud garden,
burn all of the drawing pads
that let loose portraits of her son
on my window—
and I did until
she came out screaming
at the sky to let her son go,
send him back to his room.
Then she saw me,
my face behind smoke,
my body breathing blackness.
And she began to walk
straight through until
I ran and pulled her thin body
to the ground.

4

Years later
I watched a paper boat unfold in water,
and I thought of that woman moving silently,
looking past me,
digesting stars that would never
answer her.
And I asked
what did she say when she saw him?

Perhaps she said

Nothing is real

then beat her fingers against
limbs that hung over her
as she walked through fire.

Grandfather

woke me in the middle of night
told me about 1929
child running through fields
summer blown cotton
summer blown empty cups
on dirt floors
grandfather gave me a loading zone
as if I would not have one of my own
gave me black and white pictures
circling his clock
pictures of women men smiling
with sacks near their feet
told me about the shot that killed his rabbit
but was not heard in his world
until his mother burnt herself
grabbing for the biscuits
it was '32
what band was playing
he did not know
cups of wine
came through on the radio
tin can phones
his brother calling long distance
Africa Paris London
disconnected
the line died when he stretched too far
over Egypt
'35 the rows leveled into mud
pants drying on chair backs
lye soap cleaned him good

as he soaked in the pail
cracking pecans for Sunday's pie
running through gardens
reaching for green apples
stealing red tomatoes
that hung near the dirt
his father caught him
swore him to hell
told him about his sister brother cousin
playing in ditches
catching bugs behind trees
burning them
behind a wall of dried leaves

in the middle of night
wrapped in blankets
wrapped in sleep
1929 — 1932 — 1935
he told me the river never parted

From Albert, Who Marches in Sandals on Christopher Street

Perhaps you have forgotten
how to take the calendar and dance
it on your thumb and forefinger.
Well, I haven't forgotten that dance.
Each day when those cars, long and pale,
speed past me, my feet dig
deeper into the concrete
until my toe bleeds, thick and raw
from standing in line to receive
a blessing from the city's grocery boy.
And I bleed until I
get to my job where I sign my name,
confessing I got there on time.
When I walk in, the receptionist looks
at my big swollen toe and tells me
I better take care of it quickly.
So I go in the bathroom and unwrap.
As I expect, it's all sorts of colors.
It's purple like the eye shadow that this
woman had on at last night's party,
it's blue like the food dye that kept
coming out of my mother's kitchen cabinet,
it's red like the eyes of some tired bird
who never knew when to stop flying—
There's nothing to do in looking, so
I go to work and lift those boxes from 8 to 5.
When I get home, I look
for antiseptic—or money.
But since I can't find them,

I put on my coat, go to Christopher Street
and do nothing but dance
the jig, the jig, the jig.

Junkman

I go to make my pickup,
my Thursday morning antique collecting.
And we meet again, me pulling out a broken-down
dresser to store my shorts, the flies having breakfast
on wasted food—
she was like that,
wanting whatever was left of a man,
always asking how it was when I was young,
when dreams were as certain as a
seventeenth birthday.
Playing 45s. Matching toilet tissue
with the bathroom walls.
She believed everything
had to go together and smell
like a red rose plucked from a garden.
We would dance
until the moon turned golden
and shrunk into her picture book.
We would laugh and laugh
as we hauled
wood and metal
into the truck.

You know, you have to be careful what you get.
Veneer. Junk. The kind of stuff
you buy to fill your house
with until you get rich,
all glued together, shiny, not even
scratched from a cat's paw.

You have to look at everything:
paint, color, name.
And if you got a piece of wood
that was cracked,
then you knew
you had something.
Like a chair saved from an antebellum fire,
or a music box smuggled out of a dying country
where someone spent days making that
ballerina turn on a single note. . . .
That's the kind of stuff
you polish clean; that's the kind of stuff
you take back home.

But she, she didn't want any of that.
I had to give her up
when she asked me to buy that Oriental rug.
I said no,
and then she put her face into some hard earned wrinkle,
shouting at my cracked ceiling,
letting in rain.
I left the room, and she left
some April morning, taking everything
that was new.

The Blacker the Berry,
The Sweeter the Juice

There is a blackbird in the corner,
smirking.
He's reading the newspaper, then telling me,
"The blacker the berry, the sweeter the juice,"
as I go out to get the three bags of groceries.

He does a funny dance around the
pool table,
hollering for the cue ball to stay safe—
He says he loves me,
the wind couldn't have brought him such
"a cute little thang."
He gets home at 12:01,
right after the pillow hits the door
and the pictures jump off the walls. . . .

You know, sometimes I think this blackbird
has forgotten the first minute of touch
as he moans, "baby, baby, baby."

On the Anniversary of Your Death

we forgot to clear your grave, so we stood
around talking about the bus trip,
the driver who checked his mirror to see
the cars hinging upon his line. We talked
about those who lay next to you: a
Henderson, a McCabe, a great uncle who
no one could remember anything about—we

looked for snakes. There weren't any.
And your grandchild, who could not sit
and count the statues any longer, weaved
in and out of the grass, darting through roses
that hung near his shoulders. We
called him back, but he turned his face
upward to the trees, defying all your sky—then

we remembered you:
The suit and black-feathered hat you wore
to every Wednesday night revival,
the brown shoes you polished after
you trailed the house with mud,
the nickles, the dimes, the pockets
bulging and emptying as you passed
them out before our small eyes. Your refusal
when you could not give any more.
The crying. Your wife holding your hands,
the first kiss, the second, the third, the
sheet passing over you—we

remembered. And we looked, saw
no one, except the child coming from the ditch,
trying to get back.

After the Birth

When I hold him,
I think the dead
have held the dead:
my grandmother holding
my father, a small, black
body cradled in her palm
even when her hand was stretched,
a body searching for words
between screams of hunger
that would last for fifty years,
a hunger that even she, the mother,
could not smother with her
long, dark breast.
When she looked at him,
she must have thought:
for you, no more waiting
for those plants to rise,
getting white like a cloud
cheated of rain; for you,
no more hearing that sack swing,
hoping all earth
will pull it to the ground.
She must have let him feel
fur and silk, clothes so soft
they could have been taken
from a rich woman's pillow.
And she must have told him
the history of his name:
The family who intermarried

because no other family could
take books and read them until
their eyes became hard and red,
the family that traveled down South
to fill the dirt with a kind of blackness
stolen when the moon stood
between the sun and the earth.
She must have said his name
over and over until he thought
those words were the only
words in speech.
And still, she must have held him.

Fossil

Ages later
I turn up as a fossil,
risen with Lazarus to tell
how the ground chewed my suit
until I was nothing but bone and dirt.
I hear someone say, "Bring the carbon,"
and I will confess
how the night knew my footsteps
when I only knew the roads
running into town.
I will tell them
how my mother prayed
to keep from sinning against my father
when he came home in the morning
with nothing but cool eyes
and a sack of groceries.
Then she, watching
her body grow slim,
opened her palms to me
like a bird stretching
its neck before summer.

I could do it all again:
the trick of living.
The hustle of squeezing
between a fat man and a skinny woman.
Sitting in a deli, eating a sandwich
until a waitress asks me to leave.
I could do it all again and not be
the famous, the watched, the Godzilla
stepping out of a horror movie.

I could be an animal with
leg, hand, and lung.
I don't know why they dug me up,
why they gave me this unpronounceable name,
yanked from a magician's box.
They should have been at my baptism;
heard my name shouted; seen how I thought
the river's currents would take me under
to be buried with weeds, ships, and pirates' treasures.

When they push me on this cloth,
I want to throw *them* on a slab,
cut them open to see why
they stay up all night
just to watch this pile of
porous, calcified connective tissue
blush under a revolving light.

Where are they, the scientists
urging me to speak?
They will come back and I will tell
how many people were dying,
how many put their lips to the ground. . . .
I will tell them what they want to know:
I will tell them nothing
about me.

The Monster

It got me up
right at 6:00 A.M.
Last night's excuses were not enough,
it simply said, "Get your ass up
and do some work."

I had tried to kill it
by dreaming about graduate school,
but it still came
and kicked me downstairs,
pointed to the pen, paper, and desk,
then stood behind me,
smoking cigarettes.

I told it to go
and bother the children—
you know, the ones who demand to be fed.
It wouldn't listen,
and reminded me how it consumes
flesh, bones, and fingernails.
The monster, the damn carnivore.

You know, once we were lovers.
Every night with tea, it sat with me,
said I was something, it was something,
dressed in the right clothes,
using the right words,
lovers since birth.

Since birth, then
after years of volunteer,
we became separate.
That's when the whole mess started:
the screaming upstairs, murder
plans for whoever came around me.
It wouldn't leave me alone.
Said I owed it something
for all the nights
it had listened to me
and my tales of pillow-soaked moons.

You'd think we'd be best friends by now,
forgetting the past: the heat
turned off, the bean soups and the bean salads.
But we're not, except
in that one glance when we remember
that we were both young and didn't know
that this would just become
a long understanding.

For John T. Allen, or
When a Man Can't Get to the Next Corner

John T. Allen,
you had only $3.25.
But now you are somewhere rubbing your arm,
putting alcohol on that cracked cheek,
redder now than when you went out into the cold.
Somewhere you are opening the window
to let that Melbourne Avenue light embrace you—
but you know, I never did touch you.
Remember? I had to tell you twice
to give the money up.
But you just stood there, and for a minute I thought
you were praying.
I could not believe it.
Did you think that God would remember your voice at ten?
Well, let me tell you about the time I tried
to pull that Christmas tree down,
and my Aunt Melinda wouldn't let me do it.
You see, I couldn't sleep with all those
lights blinking on and off—it was like playing
Red Light, Green Light, "Stop!" she took me
into the bathroom and pulled down my pants and touched
me until I cried "Jesus, I'm sorry!"
I prayed for her to go to hell or somewhere,
but she is still at that house pulling up her stockings
with those straps.
But sir, no one heard you.
No one thought about you.
Not even the woman around the next corner—
the corner you wanted to get to.

She was too busy counting the S&H Green Stamps
for her refrigerator. And by the next morning,
she would be in the Clark building,
filing a letter written by Anderson,
and this she knew would keep her from moving
into the stars she pulled down at night
when everything she wanted to touch
stood behind some metal door. . . .
But still, John T. Allen, when you didn't move, I
knew you had something to keep, to guard,
and hell, it wasn't the $3.25.
It was your precious voice, too sweet
to call out even when my knife
touched you, and you felt the air seeping
into your shirt. And then I just wanted to hug you,
kiss that face so still beneath me, a face
so unlike mine—the one who failed.

Song for Clara Bell

Run, run
  goes Clara Bell
    with her laughter
      in accordance with my own.
Quick, quick, yes, her mind is not at home.

Cry, cry
  goes Clara Bell
    weeping, looking for sympathy,
      cries like a spirit's moans.
Sad, sad, but her mind is not at home.

Play, play
  goes Clara Bell
    laughing with what she says
      by putting it into a lighter tone.
Funny, funny, but her mind is not at home.

Sleep, sleep
  goes Clara Bell
    scream a' many all times,
      can't leave her here alone.
Dreams, dreams, but her mind is not at home.

Sing, sing
  goes Clara Bell
    with a different melody
      this one called "Joan."
Sweet, sweet, but her mind is not at home.

Eat, eat
  goes Clara Bell
    smacking her blazing red lips
      then throwing away the bones.
Delicious, delicious, but her mind is not at home.

Hear, hear
  goes Clara Bell
    listening to the mockingbird's
      songs she has always known.
Sounds, sounds, but her mind is not at home.

Lost, lost
  is Clara Bell
    hidden in this large world
      where has Clara Bell gone?
Look, look, but her mind is not at home.

Crazy, crazy
  is my Clara Bell
    where has her mind gone?
      I just don't know.
Poor, poor, Clara Bell, her mind is not at home.

Belly Edge

When you pull the blankets over you,
you block the day, and your belly
edges the walls, hangs the picture
of the mother, the child.
When the night counsels you,
it tells you that you are
a child, even though your fingers
touch the breast
that will feed and feed
until you are empty.
To all of this you say,
Mother, it is all revelry:
this moth that follows you
as you take the streets
in daylight,
this sacrament that you have taken
to fill your body with the thought
that has kept you pressing to the water
fountain in the city,
the thought that has kept you
reaching for a drop that would
rinse your body
and have you here
in the morning rising
to take bread, juice, egg,
to pull the leg that will
kick you by noon,
to sleep for five hours, rise
for two, look in the mirror,

smile and become
the woman who will change
your husband's stillness and have him
envelop you with familiar words.
Later you say, this is a mistake.
You who were once the woman
who took fire from coals,
the woman who saw her face
burning in blue and saved it
with her own hands.
Now you think you are not
even an ember living in ash.
So for months, you pull away,
close shades to keep from watching
your stomach grow bigger,
covering the walls, covering
the bathroom mirror.
You hide until you feel
that body sink, dropping between your legs,
falling slowly into a room without light.

After Many Years of Widowhood

Husband, it is as though you interrupted
a conversation, bursting through the door
with food and wine, making me a drunkard,
like you, before slipping out again.

I keep talking to you,
dizzy, trying
to get the feel of your lips.
But I know I took your name,
believed in this ridiculousness,
had long-waisted children who are going
just as you have gone
from their mother-ghost.

I just don't know after all these years
if oxygen and water is true science,
or if I, like you,
only stumbled into the earth's laughter.

Tree Stillness

I come quietly
to see you stand over the sink,
moving your hand in water.
You cannot hear my footsteps,
even when the tree is still.

Go outside and bury the pipes,
let them lead to the ditch
and let whatever flows flow out
and sink into the dirt.
If weeds grow,
let them grow thick
until the sun burns them
on their backs,
their deaths outlined by no one.

Come, take this tree's stillness.
Forget to develop my last picture
as I will forget you
feeling the doorknob for warmth.

Pack my nightgown for someone else to slip into,
her body fitting tighter
than bones covered with dirt.

Wait for me in summer,
wait until the beaches are filled with bodies,
air filled with voices
all rising, moving in their directions.
Then you will not think
the dead only come in storms.

The Couple

In bed the woman lies,
carved out of blankets.
She turns to see
that she has placed a statue,
with immovable lips,
on the mattress.
She watches it
until it moves its hands
from left to right,
blessing the plants
whose leaves have fallen
into pots.
She says to him they are royal
lying nude upon the bed
with mohair sweaters
woven around their necks.

Black Patent Leather Shoes

Slipping into my black patent leather shoes
Not caring how many others had worn them
Or how many times they'd been
Used
Papa would make me put them on
With lace stockings
I never danced in those black leather
Shoes
Only studied their simple details:
Black
As black as my hair they surely were
With three straps, that held me there, and heels
Stacked
And I could not wear my black leather
Shoes
Every day, but only once or twice a
Week
and he would make sure black polish was
Used
Papa would make sure those shoes
Reflected me

After the Age of Thirty

I dream of machines,
emptying their memories, turning
rust like the color of old skin.
I have tried to learn
the right words, phrases, buttons,
just to become one.
In the first three months, I watched
astronauts kicking loose in space,
as TV told me these spacepeople
have the eye of a Cyclops,
focused on conquest.
I have painted my hair black
like a worn fence,
gone into stores looking
for knee-high dresses,
sat in the doctor's office
just to hear her tell me
to go back to horses,
their quiet gaits in the country,
drink well water and bathe
among rocks.
And I did until
some red roaring car—
the latest model—
came driving up to me,
snapping pictures for postcards. . . .

I went home, back to my body aching,
gliding down, trying to reshape
one last time, emptying myself
of letters, pictures, histories
before rising to meet
children dressed in tight metal.

Testament

It wasn't a good building to burn anyway:
the couch was too old,
the plaster on the floor,
baby shit and diapers everywhere.
Hell, the pipes were stolen
three years ago.
But I wanted to do something,
make the day break open twice
as people came out
with their ham and cheese sandwiches.

And I did. And it was so quiet,
peaceful, until this woman
came running out
with her hair all on fire,
falling on the cement
like some damn dog.

Motherfucker.
She wasn't supposed to have been there.
She wasn't supposed to have been called
martyr by the papers.
She never knew what was going on….

Whore, I can't
sleep at night.
Every time I roll some tobacco for a smoke,
you come wanting to sleep with me,
make me make love
and go down into your hair:
a big, red ocean.

Woman Leaving

I have packed everything:
my worn out bras kept together
by safety pins,
my slip's lace ripped out
from the bottom,
my coffee cup pieced together
with ounces of Crazy Glue.
I leave you my nightgown
to torment you,
like the ghost of a wife.
I leave you my earrings
to pierce your lobes
five times over,
my name scribbled in ink
above the toilet
to let your guest know
I have been here and left.

First Date

Behind this diamond window,
behind these lace curtains
falling to the floor,
there is something more than cigarettes,
wine sleeping in oval glasses,
stirring only between pauses—
I let you see my grandma's face
as she tried her first indoor plumbing,
disgusted at the toilet gobbling down
the toilet tissue, and her new slip
floating in water.
You laugh, but the story
isn't funny any more....
I talk about books I've heard about,
mispronouncing author and title.
My words are too simple,
and I cannot take you
to my Last Chance Baptist Church.

Talking Behind the Katydids

Talking behind the katydids,
We sleep cool tonight
In the Mississippi breeze
Under a roof of needles
Housed by cedar trees.

I never did know what Katy did
To cause so much noise.

One Mississippi, Two Mississippi

Counting the fireflies
Fireflies whispering
Around the street light.

Oh holy night!
One? Two? Group!
Thousands! Thousands!
Singing in the humid night!

Waking

Lying next to you
uncurling uncurling cover.
The morning birds
outside our stained window
nestle words in their beaks,
then speak of the storm:
trees hovering over my window
with limbs reaching
above me.
They want to come in
to see wood that once stood
with them during storms
to see the desk the chair
so warm and dry.
And the rain, the rain
dances its own dance
on my roof
while my body
stirs with the rhythm.
I hold on to you
but there is nothing in this
darkness and you do not
move to hear the water
breaking above us,
my body flooding
because I have tasted rainwater,
slept under leaves
caught bugs in cracks
and bottled those that gave off light.

I have fled many times to this house
scarf sailing in air
lightning pointing to me
as thunder burst with laughter
my lips are dry
and I am on the roof
dancing
holding on to the edge
of this hot pillow
legs pushed against the wall.
I turn once
to see the night go quickly, to see
this world awaken as I fall
deeper into the mattress.

Moments

Somehow the woman rising,
yes, the one rising to her birth morning,
peeps through the spider box, asking for more,

candles and wax.

And somehow the man in torn clothes,
yes, the one who walked cement goddesses to deserted bus stops,
dances alone to a slow rhythm, the coldness

of winter.

In October, the children bury themselves in leaves;
yes, by October, the children cover themselves with masks
and exchange names: snakes and bears slipping

into fall.

A father becomes angry with you now,
the sweat running from forehead to eye
as he sees you running to oceans

of geography.

A father walks away from you now,
not drinking sugar water, but grabbing for another beer.
He calls for his wife, swatting the flies hungry

in summer.

By the sixth year, the married watch lovers roam,
not looking at their faces, not following their footprints,
but trying to merge shadows

with shadows.

And somehow, by the sixth year, we forget Monet at galleries,
count the days of expensive flowers
and decide to buy them only for death, the pictures

of spring.

Night Rain

It pours
through the door,
and there are no sandbags
to keep it from
insisting.
The night rain moves toward me
for my second swim,
a swim where it will surround
and choose the things
that will burn
even in all of this
blue water.

Come and take me
under.
We have met before.
We have met between the
risk of drowning and the
emergence into water....
Yet, sometimes
you make me angry,
pulling me to the
bottom where I become
confused with what
you want—
a hooked death, lost rings, instances
as exact
as the ends
of a starfish.

Fool, friend, robber
I have called you when
looking through tired windows.
All these years
I have called you
night rain
under my fingers,
you who are so
unlike my first swim

when someone taught me
with lessons—
my body came up
arced like the top
of a black moon,
then I stretched out,
flapped forward
to dry towels,
afraid.

Poem for my Son

I

This is a lonely poem.
This is a poem about
water sliding over rocks, ditches,
bouncing into bubbles almost
separate from the water itself.

This is about holding
someone against your skin,
feeling every rush of air
as he peels away from you
for things that you know
will give him nothing.

II

He pushes against the floor,
and I stand staring into this hole
left open by a surgeon,
a seamstress stitching
with ill defined thread.
I want to push him back
even after his first cry.

III

If I were an artist,
I would spread
wax over you, stop

you before you put your hands
on wheels, driving
madly past apartments.
I would paint you green
like gargoyles, a Halloween treat
to keep kidnappers away, to keep
the wink from catching your eye.
I would deny you.

IV

"Cut his hair before he starts looking like a girl."
He takes the scissors;
he has done this before.
He gathers your hair from newspapers,
gives it to me to store in the
attic where it will never
turn gray
while I—I—

V

This is a poem about leaving you.
This is a poem about someone stealing your mama,
and her getting away to travel
in Maine with one suitcase
full of dancing gowns and a skinny
V-neck halter.
She's going to meet you now
on the sidewalk with a gift:
a kiss for a stranger.

For Michael

When the storm
gave me its dark clouds
for hair,
I became this black baby
lying in my mother's arms.
When the squirrels
gave me chestnuts for eyes,
I watched my body
grow nipples,
watched them grow slowly
throughout covered nights.
When I grew older,
I spoke words
that hid
behind venetian blinds.
And when I came to you, husband,
I came as a black feather
that moved against wind.

Anna, After Slavery

I ain't gonna do any mo' hoeing
I ain't gonna pick any mo' berries
get sticked and watch blood drip
over my ol' colored hands
I ain't gonna watch my granddaughter
tied to a railing whipped
her back breathin' in and out like a
baby bein' born
the sun gonna shine for me
and go down when I sez so
and I ain't gonna sing about those
fields long as the hair
swingin' from my sister's waist
I gonna plant bottle trees
an' keep dem spirits away from me
I ain't gonna be a slave no mo'
I have come back,
back like my brother
Lazarus.

You Remember the Railroad Tracks

I

You remember the railroad tracks,
the mud, the grass, the hands
that took your face and held it
against the sky.
You remember two young men
still on a thick rope, their bodies
limped, cradled by no one....
But if you had hid behind two or three
colored boys, perhaps they wouldn't have
dragged you to that tree that gathered
the sins of everything that was
black. But you didn't.
And so you wept.
A child, hair knotted with dirt.
You looked for your mother,
a washwoman with breasts dried
by the sun, a washwoman hanging
ribboned dresses on a line too far
for her to see you.
You looked for your father,
his ashy, cracked skin that rubbed
your back when you refused
to worship the delivering Jesus
who stood with stars beyond
your house.
You cried, but no one heard you
when they pushed you up
to those limbs reaching
to touch you.

II

It is twenty years later, the snow
crisscrosses above your eyes,
and inside your wife sits talking
to plants, incurable.
The fire burns and the radio
plays that old, slow music:
the piano drifting in
as horns rise to face
a cold morning.
Your wife calls you,
and when you turn to look
at the fire,
you feel the torches
surrounding you like the opening of hell.
You hear the children
shouting to see you, you the nigger
who had killed.
You did not do it.
You feel their spit, their unraveling
of legs into your stomach
as you hit the ground....
But you remember the silence,
the voice that came riding down
to let you go,, to make them disappear
as you walk back into their jail.

III

You comb your hair, look out to see the buses,
the tracks. You remember, and open the window
to the morning, to the minds elsewhere,
to the children stopping
ahead of changing lights.

"They Call it Stormy Monday,
but Tuesday's Just as Bad"

—T. Bone Walker

Sugar,

    I gotta get out of this bed.
    The piano is moaning, and the rain
    is the only water feeding us.
    The lights are off, and I can't find
    my harmonica to sing to your
    pretty black head.

Sugar,

    I'm tired of this hot dust
    powdering my face, and the
    shade trees' teasing is really
    bad. But then I think of our boy
    who knows nothing of the struggle
    Aunt Georgia had.

Sugar,

    This string guitar needs to play
    one more time. My fingers are
    aching; Memphis is 60 miles away
    and St. Lou is straight ahead, and baby

    oh baby, the flour can is empty,
    and the lard is melting like an
    avalanche of snow. When I look
    at you,

Sugar, I know the sun is climbing over our roof,
    and our Renaissance is dead.

Confession

I don't know how many times I have sinned,
or how many times I've wanted to burn
my neighbor's ass in nitric acid.
Jesus, yesterday I squeezed my son's mouth
until it was a kiss of forced passion.
He was just making noise upstairs
with his army of rubber angels,
jumping from block to block,
a heaven's descent.
Last night, I dreamed
of making love to some man.
I couldn't remember his face,
but afterwards, we stood in fire, and
I screamed at him that the Lord
punishes by hot dreams.
I woke up and saw my paycheck under light,
and I promised to give the next day.
But when the next day came,
I couldn't drop a penny into one of those plastic
"help the children" cans.
I had to buy that lipstick and eye shadow.
Lord, I went on and on, until I decided
to get myself up here because
I knew I was becoming a sinner—
but I didn't feel it.
And that's when I became scared.
I had become one of those serial killers,
traveling from Texas to California
by way of Greyhound....

Birmingham, Alabama: 1963

The choir kept singing
while the preacher screamed through the walls
Miss Anderson testified that she
was cured because she believed
and we all got the Holy Ghost
drinking his blood
eating his body
I clapped my hands and cried "Jesus!"
saw Baby sleeping on Mama's lap
his dime rolled into the aisle
"Glory!" Miss Anderson cried "Glory hallelujah!"
and then I heard a sound
saw my pink dress tear
something colored my stockings my shoes
I heard my black face split
"Mama!" I cried
and we four went up with the dust.

Don't come to this wake
or touch this small cold body
lying in velvet
I am Job's child
dead from the Lord and Satan's wager
dead when the wind closed its eyes
and smote the four corners of the house
I have been left dry
without knowing why
I have not read the papers of Birmingham.

Braid my hair
in the rain-washed morning
I want to come back to you
stand beside the stove
watch you stir steam
curl my finger around your ear
and make you hear the beating inside you
I want to breathe through the pores of this wood.

The choir keeps singing
Steal away, steal away, steal away to Jesus
the preacher keeps shouting
"So young! And she's gone!"
"Lord!" Miss Anderson cries "Lord have mercy!"
I ain't got long to stay here
Steal away, steal away home.

Frozen

As much as I hate to,
I must see the rhythm
under this ice and take
a frozen tree and make it into a gate
to keep all strangers and
cars that move so quickly out—
as if there were an out between the root
and the ground—but the root sends something
to the earth, and what we send
is something frozen: a card, a jar, a rug,
a rug to lay me down so I
might sleep in its knots.
Those knots have rhythm too.
They tie my legs to keep me from
running to the snow to tell it to
melt into water so I
might drink and live.
I cannot live with these warm hands,
so I remove my gloves, go
outside and break a piece of
ice to eat for the 9:45 dinner,
a dinner that will remind me of the snow
that hung over our house until
the school bus blew outside, picking
up all the fur-wrapped kids.
They had rhythm too.
They would run on those mirrored
sidewalks and never stop screaming—
they had something to tell that
I have forgotten to write about.
I have forgotten those

words that rise and fall
like a cardboard box sliding
down a hill. There were many hills
to climb, to lose your foot behind
rocks, or lose that ripped hat
that your mother would sew
until it was nothing but thread.
And that thread had rhythm too.
On the floor, it looked like
a snake waiting for you
to forget that it had to eat like you.
And it was like you
when you wanted to go outside.
What lies you told.

"Iforgottoasksamforthehomework
thatImissedtheday I was absent."

I am still absent, not
here. I feel the wind twirl
my scarf like it was a rope.
And the wind has rhythm too.
It bends, it pushes, it slides
between your ears
so you cannot hear the voices
speaking to you. What did they say?
Nothing. They are frozen too.
Each mumble, each whine, each "I"
lies in the slush like stiff piles
in a dirty river.
So what do you do?
You read your books;
you write the words you imagine
those people say.
But those words have rhythm too.

And you become a bird listening
to the people in the coffee shop.
They all drink coffee. It is not
too warm for them, but it makes me
remember. Like the cold that fills the
living room window, or the bomb that
someone put under my Methodist church.
They tried for five weeks
to split the Sunday school's classroom.
Someone kept telling you to get out
of that room. Get your monthly lesson
and go outside. But I could never go
outside or stay in. What was
outside the door had rhythm.
There were policemen who
marched on the street like it was
their day for parading. And there
was my sister writing everything down,
her eyes moving up and down
like the neighbor who kept running
down the steps to see what was going
on and on and on until a body swung
in jail. Hands tied. Suicide
was what they told you. And there was that
thread moving, having rhythm,
having voice. Too warm, you told them.
It was too warm. And you
went outside and marched
on the divided roads until
they told you nigger get off.
And nigger had rhythm too.
You made everyone move toward you
until they could see your brown eyes
moving like the sun
growing bigger, turning into a ball of snow.

Journey

You have been this way before:
the bus rolling in front of the drugstore;
the old men slapping their baseball hats
against each other, squatting on the sidewalks,
chewing tobacco from their tin cans.
They remember you—
yes, the one who didn't
want to watch the buildings
stay gray for twenty years;
yes, you less charitable than you are now,
as they tried to tell you how easy
it was to forget, just to forget
that they were more
than the black tar
that covered them.

Sometimes

Sometimes you want to forget
how the river mopped your floor
and took everything
a lawyer would take.
So you forget in sleep
during the afternoon's darkness,
a lamp covered with your shirt,
until the morning reminds
you that people will eventually
get in their cars
and come to see you.

Sometimes you want to tell
the ocean that it knows nothing
of your face; it cannot wash you
or seep into your kidney or your stomach
and know the thoughts that kept you
holding on to a dead bird
with black feathers.

There on the TV someone says
it is getting warmer,
but you know that even the cold
can yawn on a hot pipe.
It can breathe much better than you.
It can walk on the streets
and get nothing but
the silence it is used to.

Sometimes you want to forget
the man who said you could not do this,
could not paint a Coke can green,
you want to forget
the woman who turned your hands over
looking for likeness in your palm,
or the child that spit your way
because your hands were darker
than a cloud rising.
You want to forget your fingers
from High Ridge, Arkansas,
but you don't—
you remember the smell
of your hair washed in Delta water,
you remember the smell
of the body that covered
your eyes with handfuls of salt.

Maybe in the morning you will take
a bath towel and wring the water
for tears. And you will give
it to the girl who wants to be
a singer, so that when she stands
she feels that water rising in her throat.
She sees you holding on to tables
listening to the word she lifts out,
the word you knew
the lightness of.
It is a word that means, someone
told you to make you understand,
the sharp quills of the porcupine.
Something unbelievable.
Something you could not know
or yet draw a picture of
with fast-drying ink.

When those people come,
you take a glass and break it
in the sink, and they look
at you, perhaps thinking that you
have been up all night
counting each drop of a grasshopper's cry,
or that your tire went flat
and you were left with nothing
but a long country road and a winter coat.
But you smile and those people leave
taking nothing from you.

Sometimes you think
the ground will get tired
of taking in rain, bodies, seeds, cans,
that one day it will just say
no. That it will get up
and join the clouds and be as
far away as you are
from those people traveling
to forget the glass slivers
going down your sink.

There is a House

There is a house
that had no water running
had no tub
to hold your legs
like the faded grass
holding brown leaves sleeping
you were always sleeping
never opening your eyes
because the room would keep you
with its cracked ceiling
that you always wanted the rain
to break but it never did
you ran along
hot tarred roads
to get away from
pictures of people
you never knew or
never talked about around scattered
breakfasts of biscuits and milk
you brought from the store
who made sure your credit
was always under
they knew one day you'd be under
some dirt in the country
that holds the backroads
of Mississippi
that lead to the house
that had no water running
that you were always running from
even when you walked to
stop

Where Have the Black Sheep Gone?

for Toni Cade Bambara

Last night my daughter came to me
thin as the hands of my grandmother,
thin as the hair brushed behind
my ears when I have said
it is time to rest, it is time to rest.
She came to me and took
my black hand from the pillow,
led me to the kitchen where we
began to toast:

There was this man
who walked from Hot Coffee, Mississippi,
to Chicago. It took him 235 years,
but that man never got tired
of walking on those highways.
And when he got to Chicago, he asked
Where have the black sheep gone?
And someone told him:
They have gone grazing in the fields,
grazing on a cross that is as red as
the eyes of a drunken man.
But they like that field.
And they eat glorious.
They eat until they are as black
as a piece of night that overhangs
the city; they eat until they are as
black as the dirt that runs through
houses when the water has refused to
sink in the ground and play dead.

They eat until they are no longer
edible skin, no longer a flock of
tired meat. And the man laughed
and said, Good, let them eat until
their backs are as hard as the bones
in my hand.

And my daughter looked at me and asked,
What shall I wear?
And I said you can wear my dresses,
my stockings, my ripped blouse
that fits like the man who shakes
my hand until I forget to cry.
You can wear this black wool coat
that I wore when I went grazing
in the fields.

Visit

I

Your grandmother holds you then covers
the walls and mirrors with photos of strangers
who are, of course, kin to you.
Sometimes she tells you their names,
addresses, and the names of their children
who cry because of the heat
that goes through the uncloseable door.
She wants to snap you now,
so you line up like the lines on your forehead.
You put your hands on your hips,
and she mumbles, but takes you
looking ridiculous, ridiculous
like the heels and dress
she asks you to wear
when the wind
is undressing you roughly.

II

In the house, in a room where
you have thrown the bed covers off,
she tells you about a record
she has bought, a Christian group
that sings "Precious Jesus"
on the radio.
You think of a man
who has fever, and you twist
your hands around the bedpost,

watching her move
into her favorite corners.

III

There is a moon she praises daily,
that you see every four years
when you look at her face.
She likes her dogs, the wild
rabbit who lives in her yard.
She refuses the new house,
the bricks that scratch her hands. . . .
You do not know her age, but you have
a mother, 55, who named you.

IV

At 5:00 A.M. you tell her
it is time for you to go.
She says yes, and cooks
your breakfast on the wood stove
where iron skillets sit
too heavy for you to pick up,
or for her to give.
When you leave, she gives you
the picture that has you smiling
in the direction of trees.

Returning

I

My mother curls my hair
with smoke.
And I struggle to get
away from her legs,
away from this tin flour can
that holds me to her stomach.
Then she tells me about
the red in my black hair
that brushed against her knee
when we rode the bus to Memphis,
or about the iron
that fell on me
when I reached for her skirt.
And I move closer.

She polishes my shoes
even though I have told her
I like them dry,
caked with dirt from Missouri.
She fries fish
that swell in the black pan
like a storm that hangs outside
on cedar trees.
But I cannot eat this meal
or drink this water
she has chilled for my lips.

II

When I sleep at night
she comes to talk.
And my hair becomes gray,
then black
pressed against my head.
I go into the kitchen
dressed in a 1940 apron
she has washed
many times.
I drink her sweat,
inhale her steam.
And I say words I do not know
nor would have chosen.

III

The room shakes.
I know I must nod yes,
for this money
for our mother,
for our sister,
to the people who have kept us here
in sunken yards,
in different rooms
when we have become sick
from washing rusted pots and pans,
eating thrown away food—
sick from wanting to become flesh,
when they have become shadows.
Shadows because
they never knew us,
never had eyes nor ears
to hear the slowness

of our walk,
or see the lines
we saved every day,
after knowing the wetness
of soap.

And I cannot say no,
even though I have said no
to you before.
Mother, I have swallowed
the small pill you take
to keep your hand still
like the statue that silences museums.

The Eating Hill

Going to get some eating dirt, special dirt
For my mother.
Going to take a pail, a fork
And dig in the special ground,
Until the pail is full
With baked brown, sweet soil.

Grandma took me to the brown hill, eating hill
When I was much younger.
We the dust, ate the dirt
When very cooked
In Grandma's great oven.

Down the well, the deep well
I went to get some rainwater.
Passed lined clothes, wet clothes,
Passed great aunt's cabin
Snatching her great red rose.

Take a honeysuckle, take a blackberry,
Must take a pail of rainwater
And sit on the eating hill, special hill
Until my heart stop running,
I stop racing,
Quiet, so quiet
On the eating hill.

Closed my eyes, my brown eyes
And watched the colors bleed in darkness.
Did I hear birds? Grandma's voice?
Or was it my grasshoppers
Singing behind my shoulder?

Don't sing too loud, my Grandma's still.

"Nothing's like eating dirt,
Nothing's quick and easy to fill,"
My Grandma said, sitting on the eating hill.

Great, great, great, who?
The water restored my lips.
Remember, remember, remember when?
Grandma, you remember
Us laughing on top of
The eating hill.

My torn dress, flower dress,
Blows in my small face.
Laughing sister, younger sister,
Come to me
And let mud mix with our lace.

Cool water

Chopped wood burns
Cold rooms.
Laughing sister, sleep next to me
Living under covers.

Beans in the garden,
Oil lamps in the box,
Green leaves in my hands crumble,
Red berries grow smaller.

Too dark my dear,
My Grandma dear,
To eat with you much longer.

She is mine—
My daughter moving,
Old sister,
Old mother,
Brown-eyed dirt, lovely dirt
Waking in my arms.

Mother, mother
Grandma said
Don't take away eating dirt, special dirt
From me,
To me
Eating dirt
Would stay.

So I must climb the eating hill, special hill
In the morning.
Must walk the road, the path
Slide between trees, cedar trees
And clear caves by mid-morning.

About the Author

KAREN L. MITCHELL was born in Columbus, Mississippi, and grew up in Holly Springs, Mississippi. Her greatest ambition as a child was to be a writer and publish a book of poetry. She began writing poetry at the age of twelve, and won her first literary contest while she was in high school—the 1973 Mississippi Arts Festival Literary Competition. She received her B.A. from Stephens College, then worked in a variety of jobs—for libraries, for a historical society and for a literary magazine. She lives in Cincinnati with her children, Brock and Kyna, and her husband, Michael Collins, and is currently spending a year in Germany. This is her first book. Her next writing project might be a mystery.

ABOUT THE ARTIST

GWENDOLYN KNIGHT was born May 26, 1913 in Barbados, West Indies and moved to the United States at the age of seven. After attending Howard University, she joined Augusta Savage's workshops in Harlem. Although she is also a sculptor and writer, her main body of work is her paintings. Her work is included in collections at the Museum of Modern Art, New York City; the Seattle Arts Commission; the King County Arts Commission (Seattle); and Atlanta University. Her work has been featured internationally, in one-person and two-person exhibitions, as well as group exhibitions. The first major retrospective of her work was sponsored by the Atlanta UniversityCenter in 1988. Gwendolyn Knight lives in Seattle with her artist husband, Jacob Lawrence and is represented by Francine Seders Gallery in Seattle.

About the Book

Marcia Barrentine designed the cover for *The Eating Hill*. She is a graphic designer and artist who lives in Portland, Oregon. The text typography was composed in Palatino. The cover typography was composed in Goudy Old Style. The book was printed and bound by BookCrafters on acid-free paper. *The Eating Hill* has been issued in a first edition of fifteen hundred copies.

OTHER BOOKS FROM
THE EIGHTH MOUNTAIN PRESS

TRYING TO BE AN HONEST WOMAN
Judith Barrington
1985

COWS AND HORSES
Barbara Wilson
1988

HISTORY AND GEOGRAPHY
Judith Barrington
1989

forthcoming in the spring of 1990:

SELECTED POEMS
Irena Klepfisz
Introduction by Adrienne Rich

SELECTED ESSAYS
Irena Klepfisz
Introduction by Evelyn Torton Beck